I0505101

Investor from a young age

The importance of to start early and have time in your favor

COPYRIGHT

The rights of all texts contained in this electronic book are

reserved to its author, and are registered and protected by

copyright laws. This is an electronic edition (e-book), which

cannot be sold or marketed under any circumstances, nor used

for any purposes involving monetary interest.

If you're reading these words, it's because you're ready to take an important step towards financial freedom.

The world of investing can seem intimidating at first, but let me tell you, you're on the right track. With the right information and the right mindset, you will be able to turn your dreams into reality.

Financial freedom is more than just having money. It's about being in control of your life, being able to make decisions without worrying about running out of resources. It's the opportunity to follow your passion, build your own business, or simply enjoy life to the fullest.

But how can you achieve this financial freedom? The answer is simple: investing your money smartly and strategically. And that's exactly what this book will teach you.

You will learn the basics of investing, such as the importance of setting clear financial goals and how to create an investment plan that fits your profile. You will discover the different investment options available, from stocks to real estate funds and cryptocurrencies.

Additionally, this book will address the importance of ongoing financial education. You will learn to analyze companies and identify opportunities in the market. You will become an expert at making well-informed financial decisions.

Remember that the journey to financial freedom will not be easy. It requires dedication, patience and discipline. You'll have to take calculated risks and be prepared to face obstacles along the way.

Start with a simple step

"The journey of a thousand kilometers must begin with a single step."

This inspirational phrase by Lao Tzu perfectly captures the essence of how to start investing in the financial market.

Many people have the misconception that investing is only reserved for the rich or those who have a vast knowledge of finance. However, this limiting mindset is just a way to avoid taking the first step. The truth is that anyone, regardless of their initial capital or prior knowledge, can start investing.

All the great investors you look up to, who achieved financial independence, had to start somewhere. They took the first step, just like you can do right now.

It doesn't matter if you only have R$200 or R$200,000, the important thing is to start. The value of the initial investment is less relevant than the mindset of starting to invest.

The financial market offers a wide range of investment options, from stocks and bonds to real estate funds and cryptocurrencies. There is something for every type of investor, regardless of your preferences and financial goals.

The most important thing is to overcome fear and insecurity, understanding that the first step is essential to start your journey towards building a solid heritage. Knowledge and experience will come with time and practice.

Starting to invest does not mean that you will become an expert overnight. The important thing is to be willing to learn, research and continue to evolve. You can take advantage of available educational resources, consult experts, participate in investment courses or study groups.

Remember that every small step you take in the world of investing will bring you closer to your ultimate goal. Wealth building is a journey, not a sprint. Have patience, discipline and stay focused on long-term results.

First and second level thoughts

When it comes to investing in companies, it's important to understand the concepts of first-level and second-level thinking. These approaches help you evaluate and make informed decisions about which companies to invest in.

First-level thinking is related to the basic and superficial aspects of a company. It involves analyzing publicly available information, such as financial performance, earnings history, company reputation and market positioning. This type of analysis is critical to having an initial understanding of a company's financial health and growth potential.

Second-level thinking goes beyond basic information. It involves a deeper analysis and broader understanding of the business. This includes examining factors such as the quality of the management team, innovation and the company's ability to adapt to market changes. In addition, second-level thinking also considers the sustainability of the business model, the company's strategic positioning relative to competitors, and its ability to create long-term value.

By combining first- and second-level thinking, you can make more informed decisions and identify companies with the greatest potential for growth and financial returns. First-level analysis helps reduce risk by identifying companies with a consistent track record of financial performance. The second-level analysis allows identifying companies that have sustainable competitive advantages, innovation and solid management.

It is important to emphasize that the analysis of companies is a continuous and dynamic process. Market conditions and company fundamentals can change over time. Therefore, it is essential to regularly monitor and update your analysis and make investment decisions based on the most recent information available.

Remember that the combination of first and second level thinking allows you to take a more complete and informed view when investing in companies. This helps to minimize risks and increase the chances of obtaining satisfactory financial returns over time.

The investment world

Have you ever stopped to think about the power money can have? He can open doors, provide financial freedom and make dreams come true. And one of the most effective ways to make your money work for you is through investing.

Getting started in the world of investing is like opening a door to a universe of opportunities. It's like discovering a new way to multiply your resources and achieve financial independence.

However, many people are intimidated by the idea of investing. They think it's complicated, restricted only to financial market specialists. But I'm here to tell you that's not true.

Investing can be simple and affordable for everyone. You don't need to be a financial whiz to get started. All you need is knowledge and a willingness to learn.

By venturing into the world of investing, you will be putting your money to work for you. And that's awesome because it means you're building a financially strong future for yourself.

Imagine the feeling of seeing your money grow, reaching financial goals and having more confidence to face life's challenges. With investments, you can make your dreams come true and live the life you've always wanted.

But remember: investing requires discipline and patience. It is not about getting rich overnight, but about a path to be followed with strategy and caution.

self education

Formal education is essential to acquire skills and knowledge needed for the job market. It opens doors, offers opportunities and can ensure a financially stable life. However, if you want to achieve an extraordinary level of financial success, you need to go further.

Self-education is the secret to achieving a fortune. It is the act of seeking knowledge beyond the confines of the classroom, delving into specific areas of interest and constantly keeping up to date on financial market trends.

To stand out in the world of investments, it is essential to constantly study. Consume good content, such as books, articles, podcasts and online courses that address topics relevant to the financial market. Learn from experts, follow economic news and always be willing to explore new strategies and approaches.

However, just accumulating theoretical knowledge is not enough. Self-education also involves putting into practice what you have learned. Review investment opportunities, make informed decisions and be willing to take calculated risks. Apply the knowledge gained to build a solid and profitable investment portfolio.

Self-education has no limits. It doesn't matter your age, experience or starting point. You can start today to seek knowledge, develop skills and become a successful investor.

So, stop settling for the formal education that allows you to earn a living. Pursue the self-education that will enable you to achieve a fortune. Invest in yourself, in your knowledge and in your personal development. The financial return and the realization of your dreams are waiting for you.

Remember Jim Rohn's words and turn them into action. Embrace the journey of self-education, be open to learning, be persistent and never stop developing. You are in control of your financial future and you can achieve an extraordinary life.

So, start investing in your education right now. The great

fortune you desire is just one step beyond your comfort zone.

Investor mindset from a young age

Developing an investor mindset from a young age is one of the most important steps you can take towards a prosperous financial future.

It's like planting a seed that will grow and bear fruit throughout your life. Let's explore the importance of this mindset and how it can positively impact your financial journey.

Investing at a young age offers a number of valuable benefits. First, it lets you learn about the power of money and how to make it work for you. By understanding the basics of investing, you will have the ability to make informed, strategic decisions to grow your wealth over time.

Additionally, developing an investor mindset early on provides valuable financial education. You'll learn about the different types of investments available, such as stocks, bonds, mutual funds, and real estate, among others. This will give you a comprehensive understanding of financial markets and help you make informed decisions about where to allocate your money.

An investor mindset from a young age also teaches important lessons about patience, discipline and perseverance. Investing is not a quick path to instant wealth, but a long-term journey. By starting early, you'll learn how to set realistic goals, create a solid investment plan, and stay committed in the face of obstacles.

Another crucial aspect is the power of time and the effect of compound interest. By starting your investments at a young age, you will have the advantage of allowing your money to grow over many years. Even small initial investments can turn into significant sums over time, thanks to the power of compound interest.

Developing an investor mindset early on also opens the door to greater financial independence and freedom. By building a diverse and smart portfolio, you'll be creating a solid foundation to reach your financial goals, such as buying a home, starting a business or fulfilling personal dreams. This financial independence will allow you to have more control over your life and make decisions based on your values and aspirations.

So don't underestimate the power of developing an investor mindset from a young age. Start today, even if it's with small steps. Learn about the investment world, seek knowledge, talk to experienced people and, above all, start taking action. Every financial choice you make now will have a significant impact on your future.

Remember that the investment journey is a marathon, not a sprint. Stay committed, learn from mistakes, adjust your strategy when necessary, and above all, never stop learning. The investor mindset is a powerful tool that will accompany you throughout your life, enabling you to achieve financial freedom and fulfill your dreams. So start developing this mindset today and walk a path towards a prosperous and abundant financial future.

NOP technique (Notice, Listen, Practice)

Developing an Investor Mindset from a Young Age:

Uses:

Financial Self-Awareness: Start by developing a clear awareness of the importance of finance and investing in your life. Recognize that an investor mindset from a young age can have lasting benefits for your financial future.

Opportunities Around You: Be aware of opportunities for learning and financial growth around you. Look at the success stories of young investors and entrepreneurs. Realize that you too can walk this path and achieve financial freedom.

To hear:

Seek Mentors: Look for mentors or people experienced in the field of investing. Listen to their advice and learn from their experiences. Be willing to absorb valuable knowledge and insights that can help you develop a young investor mindset.

Learn from the Experts: Consume educational content about investments and finance. Follow books, blogs, podcasts and videos from renowned experts in the field. Be open to different perspectives and investment strategies.

To practice:

Start with Small Investments: Take the first step by investing even with modest amounts. Open an account at a brokerage firm, choose an investment suited to your profile and start putting the acquired knowledge into practice. Constant practice will allow you to gain experience and confidence over time.

Reevaluate and Adjust: Be willing to reevaluate and adjust your investment strategies as you gain more knowledge and experience. Watch your investments perform, learn from your mistakes, and make adjustments as needed. This will help you to continually improve your young investor mindset.

Remember that developing a youth investor mindset is an ongoing process. By noticing opportunities, listening to valuable advice, and practicing the concepts learned, you'll be well on your way to cultivating a solid investor mindset and achieving financial independence early on. Stay committed, stick with your journey, and remember that every step you take toward an investor mindset is an investment in yourself and your financial future.

Risk

The concept expressed by Warren Buffett, one of the most renowned investors in the world, is direct and impactful: "Risk comes from not knowing what you are doing." This phrase is an important lesson for young investors, highlighting the importance of financial knowledge and education in making investment decisions.

In simple terms, risk refers to the possibility of losing money or not getting the expected results from an investment. Warren Buffett points out that this risk is directly related to the lack of knowledge and understanding of the investment in question. If you don't know what you're doing, if you don't have enough information about the market, the companies or the assets you're investing in, the chances of making wrong decisions and facing financial losses increase significantly.

For young investors, this phrase is a powerful reminder that investing is not just a matter of luck or intuition, but requires a grounded and informed approach. It is essential to seek knowledge and understanding about the investments you want to make. This includes understanding how financial markets work, learning about different types of assets, analyzing company fundamentals, and knowing the basics of valuing investments.

By gaining knowledge and educating yourself financially, you will be increasing your chances of making informed investment decisions and minimizing the risks involved. Warren Buffett, with his vast investment experience and success, emphasizes the importance of knowing what you are doing to avoid unnecessary risks and maximize return opportunities.

Therefore, for young investors, the central message is clear: invest time and effort in your financial education. Learn as much as you can about the investments that interest you. Be prepared to carry out careful analyzes and make decisions based on solid facts and information. By doing so, you will be reducing the risks associated with investing and building a strong foundation for achieving your long-term financial goals. Remember that knowledge is a powerful tool that will allow you to confidently navigate the investment world and pursue

financial success.

Immediacy kills anyone

In the fast-paced world we live in, it is common for young people to be more immediate in their expectations and desires. The quest for quick results and instant gratification is a natural feature of this phase of life. However, when it comes to investing, it is essential to learn to be patient and understand that the game is soon.

Investing successfully requires understanding that significant returns often come over time, not instantaneously. It takes patience to wait for investments to grow, allowing the power of compound interest and time to work in your favor.

Young people have a unique advantage when it comes to investing: time. Time is one of an investor's greatest allies, as it allows investments to grow and appreciate over the years. By starting investments early, young people have the opportunity to reap the benefits of long-term growth and build a strong foundation for the future.

It is essential to understand that the investment game is soon, but that does not mean that you need to act impulsively or seek immediate results. On the contrary, it is necessary to develop a long-term mindset and resist the temptation to seek quick and speculative gains.

By cultivating patience in investing, you will be taking a disciplined and strategic approach. This involves making decisions based on sound analysis, diversifying investments and staying committed to your long-term financial goals. Patience allows you to go through periods of volatility without letting yourself be shaken, understanding that it is part of the game and that, in the long run, the results tend to be positive.

Diversification

In essence, diversifying means not putting all your eggs in one basket. Rather, it's spreading your investments across different asset classes such as stocks, bonds, real estate and others, as well as across different economic sectors. By doing so, you are spreading risk more evenly, avoiding over-reliance on a single investment or specific industry.

Imagine the following situation: you decide to invest all your savings in a single company. While the company may be doing well right now, there are a number of external factors that can affect its performance, such as changes in the market, fierce competition, or even internal problems within the company. If something negative happens, you will be subject to huge financial losses.

On the other hand, if you diversify your investments, you will be building a portfolio that benefits from different opportunities and faces risks more evenly. If one asset class is not doing so well, another may be performing better, helping to offset any losses.

Diversification not only reduces risk, it also increases your chances of earning consistent returns. By investing in different assets and sectors, you are taking advantage of growth opportunities in various areas of the economy. While some investments may go through low times, others may be on the rise, ensuring greater stability and balance in your portfolio.

Remember that diversification isn't just about spreading your investments around randomly, it's about performing careful analysis and making informed decisions. Try to understand the different assets, sectors and their interactions with the market. Seek guidance from qualified professionals or study on your own to make informed decisions.

As a young investor, you have the advantage of having time on your side. Take this opportunity to build a diversified portfolio and adapt it over time, according to your goals and changes in

the economic scenario. Remember that diversification is a

long-term strategy, and positive results will come with time.

How to Read Charts If You're New to the Market

If you are new to the financial market and are starting to get familiar with reading charts, it is important to understand some basic concepts in order to correctly interpret the information presented. Here are some tips to help you through this process:

Choose the right chart type: There are different types of charts such as line charts, bar charts and candlestick charts. Each of them provides information in a different way. Start with a simple line graph that shows price changes over time.

Identify the axes: Charts have horizontal and vertical axes. The horizontal axis represents time, with dates or periods indicated. The vertical axis shows price or percentage change. Familiarize yourself with the scale used on the vertical axis to understand the magnitude of price changes.

Analyze trends: Observe whether the chart shows an upward (bullish), downward (bearish) or sideways trend (no clear trend). Identifying trends is important for making buy or sell decisions.

Use Technical Indicators: Technical indicators such as moving averages, MACD and RSI help to identify hidden patterns and trends in charts. They can provide additional information about opportune times to enter or exit a position.

Watch price patterns: Some common price patterns, such as support, resistance, and trend lines, can give you clues about upcoming market moves. Learn to identify these patterns and use them in your analyses.

Use different timeframes: Analyze the same asset on different time frames, such as daily, weekly and monthly charts. This will help to get a bigger picture and identify longer-term trends.

Take notes and record your observations: Keep an investment journal to record your analyses, decisions and results. This will help you learn from your experiences and improve your analytical skills.

Remember that reading charts is a skill that takes practice and experience. As you become familiar with different chart elements and patterns, your ability to interpret them will improve. Also, don't forget to combine technical analysis with fundamental analysis, also considering company fundamentals and relevant economic events.

investment horizon

The investment horizon is the length of time you plan to hold your investments. It is important to define your investment horizon to guide your asset and strategy choices.

If you have a short investment horizon, it means that you plan to redeem your investments in a period of a few months to a few years. In this case, it is important to consider more liquid and lower risk assets that can be quickly converted into cash, if necessary. Some examples are short-term fixed income investments, such as Direct Treasury bonds with shorter maturities, or short-term investment funds.

The long-term investment horizon involves the intention to hold your investments for several years, possibly decades. With a longer horizon, you can take a little more risk in pursuit of higher returns. In this case, it may be interesting to consider investments in stocks of companies with a good track record of performance and long-term growth potential, or even investments in real estate.

It is important to remember that the investment horizon is not a fixed rule, and can be adjusted over time according to your needs and objectives. For example, if you plan to buy a home five years from now, you may need to adjust your investment horizon for that specific period.

When defining your investment horizon, consider your financial goals and your future needs. Consider factors such as redemption deadlines, risks involved and the return potential of the different assets available. Remember that time is a powerful investment ally, allowing you to benefit from the growth and appreciation of your investments over the years.

Therefore, when planning your investments, consider your investment horizon. Whether short, medium or long term, this definition will help guide your choices and strategies, ensuring that your investments are aligned with your financial goals and future needs.

managing risks

As you begin your journey into the investment world, it is essential to understand the importance of risk management.

While the idea of taking risks may sound exciting, it's crucial to keep in mind that making informed financial decisions and protecting your wealth are equally important aspects.

Risk management refers to identifying, assessing and controlling the risks associated with your investments. Every investment carries some level of risk, and it is critical to understand the different types of risks involved and implement strategies to mitigate them.

One of the first steps in risk management is to diversify your investment portfolio. By spreading your resources across different assets, sectors and regions, you reduce exposure to a single investment. That way, even if an investment does not show the expected results, others can offset losses and keep your portfolio balanced.

Furthermore, it is important to carry out a careful analysis before making any investment decisions. Knowing the characteristics of the assets you are investing in, such as their performance history, future prospects, volatility and liquidity, will help you make more informed decisions and reduce the risk of significant losses.

Another effective risk management strategy is to set a limit on the amount you are willing to lose on your investments. This is known as a "stop loss", which is a predetermined point at which you decide to sell an asset if it falls below this value. This technique helps limit your losses and protect your equity.

It is critical to stay up-to-date on changes in the market and the economy. Follow financial news, study market movements and seek guidance from qualified professionals. This will help you to identify and assess emerging risks, allowing you to make more informed and informed investment decisions.

Risk management does not mean completely avoiding risk, but controlling it and making it more manageable. Investing involves uncertainties, but with good risk management, you will be able to make more balanced decisions and minimize possible losses.

So this is an essential part of the investment journey. By understanding the risks involved, diversifying your portfolio, performing careful analysis and making informed decisions, you will be protecting your equity and increasing your chances of achieving positive results. Remember that investing is a marathon, not a sprint, and risk management is the key to a safer and more prosperous financial journey.

We all need mentors

When embarking on a journey into the investment world, it is critical to recognize the importance of finding mentors. These experienced guides play a key role in your financial journey, providing valuable insights and practical guidance.

Mentors are individuals who have already walked the path you want to walk. They have experience and wisdom accumulated over the years of working in the financial market. By seeking out mentors, you have the unique opportunity to learn from their experiences and valuable advice.

One of the main advantages of having a mentor is being able to learn from his mistakes and successes. They can share their experiences, reveal pitfalls to avoid, and provide insight into effective investment strategies. By leveraging the mentor's knowledge, you gain a significant advantage in making financial decisions.

Additionally, a mentor can offer emotional support and encouragement along your journey. Investing can be challenging, and having the support and motivation of someone with experience can be extremely valuable.

Another benefit of having a mentor is the opportunity to expand your network. Your mentor likely has a wide network of relationships in the investment world. These connections can open doors, provide learning opportunities, and even lead to profitable partnerships. Take this opportunity to build valuable relationships and learn from influential professionals.

Finding a mentor doesn't mean relying exclusively on them. You remain responsible for your own decisions and investments. The mentor is there to offer guidance and support, but it's up to you to make the final decisions.

As an investor looking to succeed, you have the advantage of being able to find mentors willing to share their expertise. Many experienced professionals are willing to help younger people, inspired by the energy and enthusiasm of youth. Therefore, do not hesitate to look for mentors at events, lectures or through online platforms. Be open and prepared to learn from those who have already walked the path you want to take.

Remember that seeking a mentor is a valuable investment in yourself. Learning from the experiences of others, receiving expert guidance and building meaningful relationships are essential elements for your growth and success in the investment world.

So be proactive, persistent and open to opportunities that arise. Find a mentor who can guide you on your journey to financial success. With the right guidance, you'll be on your way to achieving greater levels of knowledge, skills and financial prosperity.

Move forward with determination in your search for mentors, and write your success story alongside those who will guide you towards the financial freedom you so desire.

money is patience

There is a famous phrase that says: "The market takes money from the impatient and gives it to the patients". This statement perfectly sums up the importance of patience in the investment world.

The stock market is a dynamic and unpredictable environment where stock prices can fluctuate quickly and significantly. Often, impatient investors are attracted by the idea of making quick profits and end up making hasty decisions based on momentary emotions. And that's when the market can take money from these investors.

Patient investors, on the other hand, have a different mindset. They understand that investing in stocks is a long-term journey and that consistent returns come with time. These investors have the ability to weather daily market swings and not get carried away by short-term trends.

Patience in the stock market is related to sound investment strategies and discipline. Patient investors know that it is necessary to do a careful analysis of companies, understand their fundamentals and long-term perspectives. They are willing to wait for the right time to buy quality stocks and have the composure needed to hold onto their investments even during periods of volatility.

That patience pays off over time. Patient investors are more likely to take advantage of bull market cycles, reaping the rewards of their long-term investments. They trust their strategies and are not shaken by daily ups and downs.

So if you want to be successful in the stock market, developing a patient mindset is critical. Learn to control your emotions, avoid making impulsive decisions based on momentary information, and be confident in your long-term investment strategy.

Remember that investing in stocks is not a get rich quick scheme. It is a journey that requires time, knowledge and patience. Those who are able to cultivate patience are the ones most likely to earn solid, lasting returns.

Be patient, stay focused on your long-term goals, and let the market reward your patience over time. The stock market can take money from the impatient, but it is ready to reward handsomely those who are patient and disciplined in their approach to investing.

How to analyze companies to invest in

Business analysis is a key step in investing wisely and minimizing risk. By carefully evaluating companies, you will be able to identify those that have the potential for growth, profitability and financial strength. Here are some steps to review companies and make informed investment decisions:

Assess financial health: Check key financial indicators such as revenues, profits, cash flow and debt. Review the company's financial reports to understand its ability to generate consistent profits over time.

Analyze the industry and competition: Understand the context in which the company operates. Assess industry dynamics, existing competition, and market trends. This will help you identify whether the company is well positioned to take advantage of opportunities and address challenges.

Study the growth history: Check the company's history in terms of revenue growth, profits and market value. This will provide insights into your ability to expand and generate returns in the future.

Review Management: Assess the company's management team, including their background, experience, and track record. Competent leadership aligned with the interests of shareholders is a key factor for long-term success.

Examine the business strategy: Understand the company's strategy to stand out in the marketplace. Assess whether the company has a sustainable competitive advantage and is efficiently pursuing growth opportunities.

Consider the fundamentals: Analyze the company's fundamentals, such as the intrinsic value of its shares, the price-to-earnings ratio and other relevant indicators. This information will help you determine whether the company's stock is undervalued or overvalued in the market.

Assess dividend potential: If you are interested in investments that pay dividends, check the company's profit distribution policy. Evaluate whether the company has a consistent history of paying dividends and whether there are prospects for growth in these payments.

Remember that business analysis is an ongoing process. As you gain more knowledge and experience, you will be able to improve your analysis skills and make more informed decisions. Also, consider diversifying your investments, spreading your capital across different companies and sectors, to reduce risk and increase the chances of achieving consistent returns.

More constant, less intense

When it comes to investing, many believe that intensity is the key factor in achieving financial success. However, it's important to remember that constancy plays a much more significant role in your investment journey.

Constancy is the act of maintaining a disciplined and consistent approach over time. This means making regular investments, regardless of market fluctuations or economic circumstances. While intensity is related to acting with fervor and emotion, constancy involves an ongoing commitment and a long-term view.

Constancy is important because the financial market is volatile and unpredictable. Stock prices can rise and fall on a daily basis, and it is impossible to accurately predict the ideal time to buy or sell. Those who try to hit the market with intense moves run the risk of making impulsive decisions that are detrimental to their investments.

On the other hand, constancy allows you to harness the power of compound growth over time. Investing regularly, even in small amounts, allows you to build equity consistently. Constancy also reduces the effects of market fluctuations, as you will be buying assets at different times, taking advantage of both bullish and bearish periods.

Also, constancy is a demonstration of discipline and emotional control. Maintaining a constant investment strategy and resisting the temptation to make decisions based on momentary emotions are essential characteristics of a successful investor. Constancy helps you avoid common mistakes, such as buying at the top of the market or selling during a temporary dip.

By adopting constancy in your investments, you develop a valuable habit of saving and investing, building your wealth sustainably over time. Regardless of market fluctuations, you continue to invest regularly, confident in your long-term strategy and goals.

So remember that constancy is more important than intensity when it comes to investing. Cultivate the habit of investing regularly, regardless of the circumstances, and stick to your long-term strategy. Consistency will allow you to enjoy the benefits of compound growth and reduce the risks associated with intense and emotional movements.

Be constant, stay focused and persevere in your investment journey. In time, you will reap the rewards of your efforts, achieving greater financial stability and creating a prosperous future for yourself. Constancy is the key to successful investing and a solid foundation for building long-term wealth.

not everything can be bought

"It's good to have money and everything money can buy, but it's also good to have a checkup every now and then to make sure you haven't missed the things money can't buy."

The concept expressed in this sentence is that having money and enjoying the material benefits it provides is important, however, it is equally crucial to value and preserve the things that money cannot buy.

Often, we focus so much on accumulating wealth and achieving financial success that we overlook essential aspects of life that cannot be purchased with money. These things include loving relationships, health, happiness, peace of mind, time with family and friends, meaningful experiences, and emotional well-being.

By incessantly seeking material wealth, we run the risk of losing sight of the true purpose of life. We can sacrifice our health, neglect important relationships, and live in constant stress and anxiety, all in pursuit of more money. However, there comes a time when we realize that these things cannot be bought, and the lack of them can leave a void in our lives.

That's why it's essential to do a periodic "check-up", an honest assessment, to ensure that we haven't lost or neglected the valuable things that money can't provide. This checkup involves reflecting on our priorities, balancing our financial struggles with our personal relationships, health and emotional well-being, and reassessing whether we are living a truly fulfilling and fulfilling life.

Valuing what money can't buy reminds us of the importance of finding balance in our quest for wealth and success. It means cultivating healthy and meaningful relationships, taking care of our physical and mental health, dedicating time to activities that bring us joy and allow us to grow as individuals.

While it's nice to have money and enjoy the material benefits it brings, we must always remember that true wealth lies in the things that cannot be bought. By doing this check-up regularly, we make sure we are living a balanced and meaningful life, valuing both the financial achievements and the emotional gems that bring us true happiness and satisfaction.

save more

"If you aim to be rich, think of saving as you think of earning (money)."

This concept expresses the importance of saving and not just focusing on earning money to achieve wealth. Often, when we think about improving our financial situation, we focus our attention on increasing our income, looking for opportunities to earn more and looking for additional sources of income. However, saving is an essential element in this process.

Saving means setting aside a portion of the money we receive and not spending it right away. It is an act of financial discipline that allows us to accumulate resources for the future and create a solid foundation for building long-term wealth.

The concept underscores that just as we strive to earn money, we should have the same mindset and dedication to saving.

Saving should not be seen as a secondary or optional act, but as a fundamental strategy to achieve wealth and financial stability.

By thinking about saving as much as we think about earning, we recognize the importance of controlling our expenses, avoiding waste and directing a part of our money to investments, savings or long-term plans. It's a mindset that reminds us that every penny saved today can become a source of growth and financial security in the future.

Saving allows us to face financial emergencies, carry out personal projects and goals, invest in lucrative opportunities and achieve financial independence. In addition, saving gives us a sense of tranquility and freedom, knowing that we have a reserve to face unforeseen events and take advantage of the opportunities that arise along the way.

Therefore, if we aim at wealth, we must attach as much importance to saving as we do to earning money. A saving mindset empowers us to create a strong financial future, develop healthy money management habits, and move closer to our financial goals. By balancing the increase in our income with a consistent practice of saving, we are building the foundations for a prosperous and stable financial life.

Never spend your money before you own it.

This concept emphasizes the importance of having a responsible attitude towards money, avoiding spending it before actually having it. It's a powerful reminder to act with financial prudence and avoid falling into the traps of debt and financial mismanagement.

We are often tempted to spend beyond our means, driven by the expectation of future earnings or the illusion that money will come easily. However, this mentality can lead to serious financial consequences, such as excessive debt, lack of resources to cover basic expenses and an unstable financial life.

By spending money we don't yet have, we are compromising resources that haven't yet been acquired. We are anticipating the use of future resources, running the risk of not being able to meet our financial commitments or achieve our long-term financial objectives.

The concept reminds us of the importance of living within our means, spending based on our current income rather than future expectations. It means being aware of our financial limitations and making spending decisions based on a realistic assessment of our current situation.

By adopting this mindset, we protect our financial stability and ensure the ability to handle unforeseen events and unexpected expenses. Plus, we avoid the pressure and stress that comes with debt and financial imbalance.

Therefore, it is essential to exercise financial prudence and never spend money before you have it. That means prioritizing building a solid financial foundation, setting a realistic budget, saving to meet goals, and avoiding unnecessary debt accumulation.

By adopting this approach, we are cultivating a healthy relationship with money, based on responsibility and the pursuit of a stable and balanced financial life. Remember: it's better to wait, save and achieve what you want than to risk your financial stability and well-being by spending beyond your means.

Conclusion

Throughout this material, we explore several concepts and strategies that are fundamental for those who wish to walk the path of financial independence. We learned about the importance of developing an investor mindset from a young age, seeking financial education and finding mentors who can guide us on this journey.

We discovered the relevance of investment diversification, risk management and the investment horizon. We learned that patience, constancy and emotional control are virtues that we must cultivate to be successful in the financial market. We understand that money must be used wisely, avoiding impulsive and anticipated spending, and prioritizing savings as the basis for building wealth.

Now, more than ever, is the time to put the acquired knowledge into practice. It's time to take charge of our financial lives, look for investment opportunities, plan for the future and work towards financial freedom. Every step we take towards that goal brings us closer to fulfilling our dreams and puts us in control of our own destiny.

The investment journey is not a sprint but a marathon. It takes perseverance, discipline and determination to achieve significant results over time. Stay true to your goals, learn from mistakes, adapt to market changes and never stop seeking knowledge.

Don't let circumstances or immediacy take away the opportunity to build a solid foundation of prosperity.

Take advantage of this knowledge, take control of your financial life and walk towards freedom and prosperity. You have the potential to achieve great things.

www.ingramcontent.com/pod-product-compliance
Lightning Source LLC
Chambersburg PA
CBHW070826220526
45466CB00002B/762